PIANO • VOCAL • GUITAR

josh Groban

Photography: Jay Blakesberg

Italian text edited by Marco Marinangeli
Magelic Productions Inc.

ISBN-13: 978-1-4234-2462-8
ISBN-10: 1-4234-2462-X

HAL•LEONARD® CORPORATION

7777 W. BLUEMOUND RD. P.O. BOX 13819 MILWAUKEE, WI 53213

Visit Hal Leonard Online at
www.halleonard.com

D1294201

contents

alla luce del sole 6

gira con me 11

you're still you 16

cinema paradiso (se) 28

to where you are 32

alejate 21

canto alla vita 38

let me fall (from cirque du soleil) 44

vincent (starry, starry night) 48

un amore per sempre 52

home to stay 57

jesu, joy of man's desiring 62

the prayer 69

ALLA LUCE DEL SOLE

Words and Music by MAURIZIO FABRIZIO
and GUIDO MORRA

*Original recording in A♭ minor.

GIRA CON ME

Words and Music by WALTER AFANASIEFF,
DAVID FOSTER and LUCIO QUARANTOTTO

Bridge:

Chorus:

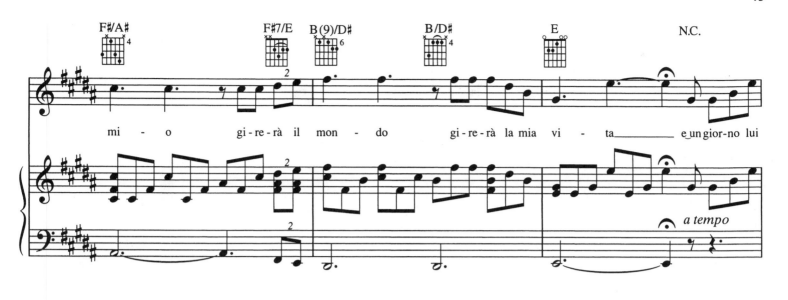

mi - o gi-re-rà il mon-do gi-re-rà la mia vi - ta_____ e un gior-no lui

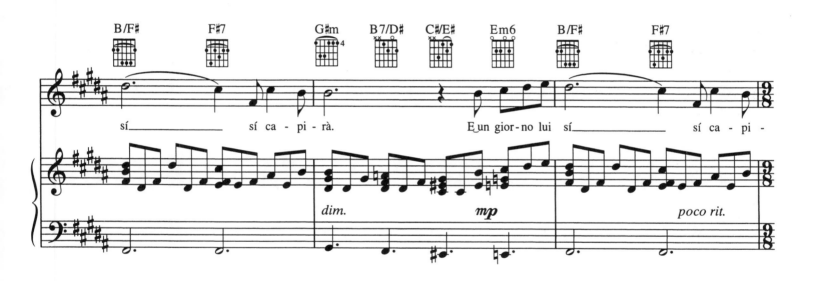

sí_____ sí ca - pi - rà. E un gior-no lui sí_____ sí ca - pi -

rà._____

YOU'RE STILL YOU

Words by LINDA THOMPSON
Music by ENNIO MORRICONE

Slowly, with expression ♩=76

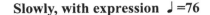

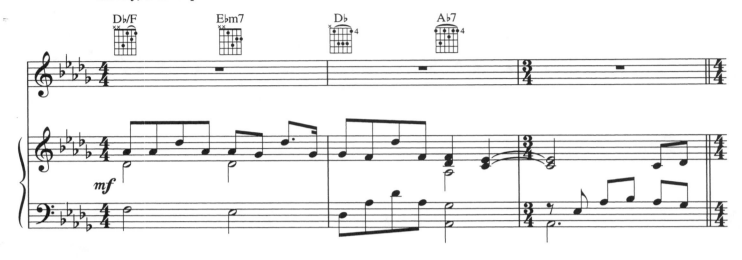

Verse 1:

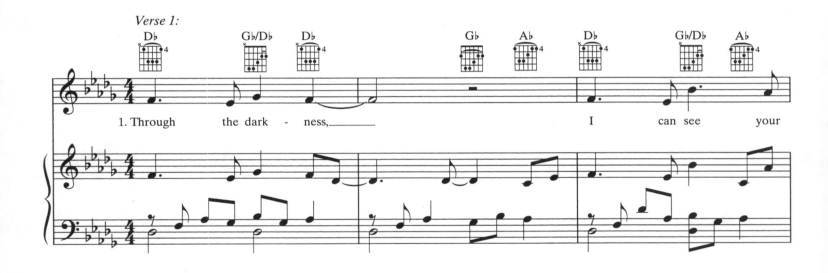

1. Through the dark - ness, ___ I can see your

light. And you will al - ways shine, and I can feel your

af - ter all is said and done, you're still you. Af - ter

all, you're still you.

Verse 2:

2. You walk past me._____ I can feel your

pain. Time chang - es ev - 'ry - thing. One truth al - ways

stays the same: You're still you. Af-ter all, you're still

you. *Verse 3:* 3. I look up to____

____ ev-'ry-thing you____ are.____

In my eyes you do no wrong._____ And I be-lieve in you, al-

ALÉJATE

Words and Music by ALBERT HAMMOND,
MARTI SHARRON and CLAUDIA BRANT

1. Ja - más sen - tí en el al - ma tan - to a - mor, y

na - die mas que tù me a - mò; por ti reí y llo - ré,

re - na - cí y cam - bié, lo que tu - ve dí por te - ner - te a - quí. Ya

CINEMA PARADISO

Music by ENNIO MORRICONE

Moderately slow, with expression ♩ = 66

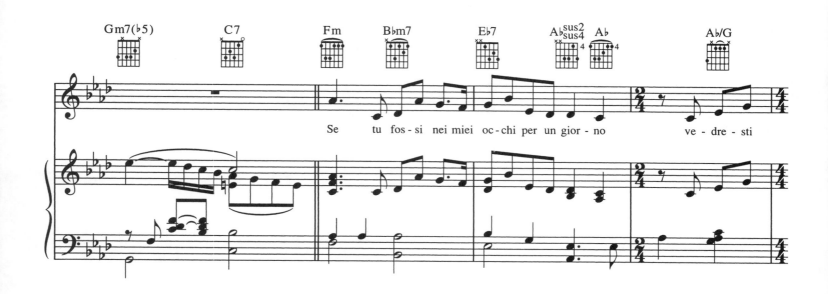

Se tu fos-si nei miei oc-chi per un gior - no ve - dre - sti

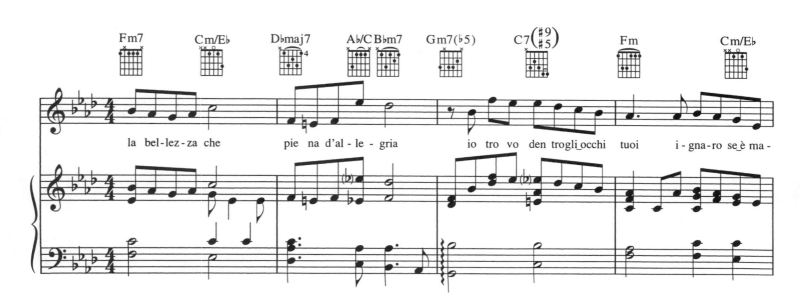

la bel-lez-za che pie na d'al - le - gria io tro vo den trogli occhi tuoi i - gna-ro se è ma-

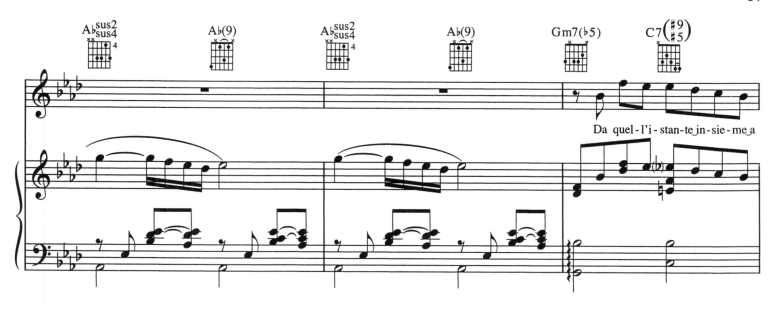

Da quel - l'i - stan - te_in - sie - me_a

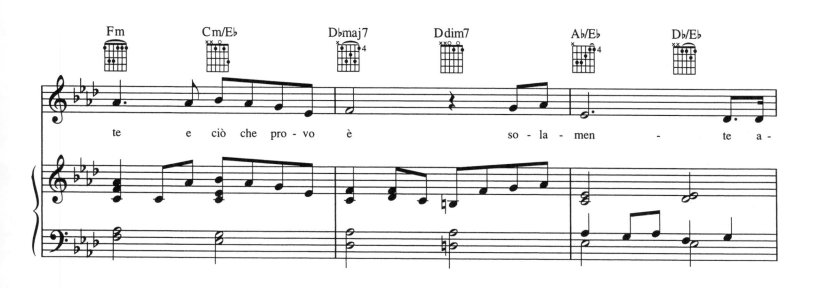

te   e ciò che pro - vo   è   so - la - men - te   a -

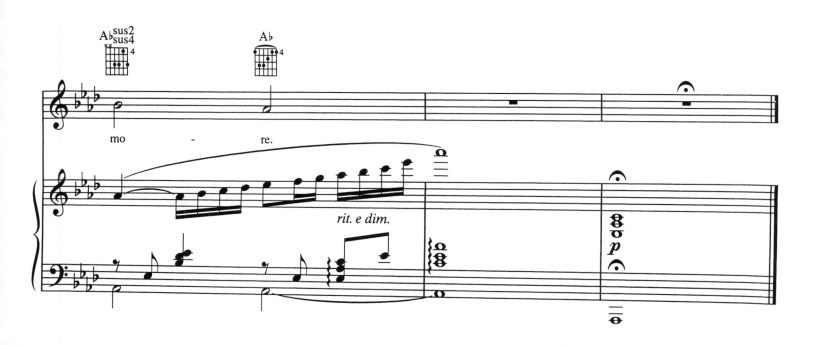

mo - re.

rit. e dim.

TO WHERE YOU ARE

Words and Music by LINDA THOMPSON
and RICHARD MARX

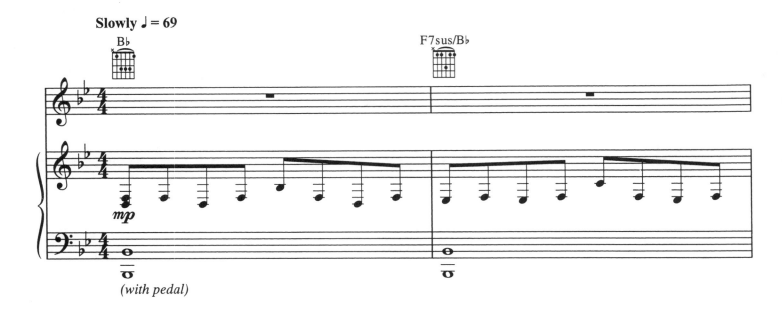

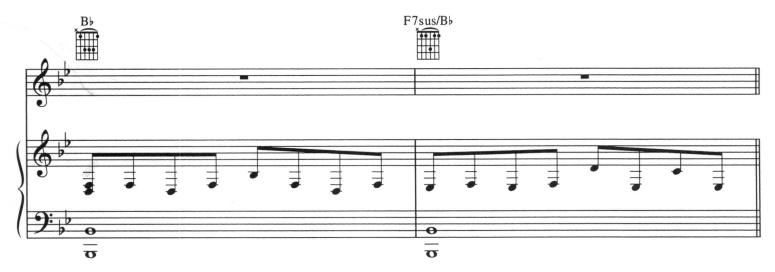

watch-ing o - ver me___ from up a - bove?

% *Chorus:*

Fly___ me up___ to where___ you are___ be - yond___ the dis - tant

star I wish up - on___ to - night___ to see you smile, if

on - ly for___ a while___ to know___ you're there. A

Verse 2:

breath a - way's__ not far to where you are.__

2. Are you gen - tly sleep - ing here in - side my dream?__ And

is - n't faith__ be - liev - ing all pow - er can't__ be seen?

As my heart holds__ you just one beat a - way, I

cher - ish all___ you gave___ me ev - 'ry day. 'Cause you are

my for - ev - er love watch - ing

me from up a - bove. And I be -

lieve that an - gels breathe and that

CANTO ALLA VITA

Words and Music by GIUSEPPE DETTORI,
ANTONIO GALBIATI and ALFREDO RAPETTI

De-di-ca-to a chi col-pe-vole_o in-no-cen-te per-so_in que-sto ma-re si_è ar-

re-so_al-la cor-ren-te a chi non è mai sta-to vin-cen-te.

Chorus:

Non du-bi-ta-re mai, non du-bi-ta-re mai tu

(Ci chia - ma.)

non la-sciar-la mai da so - la, da so - la, an-co - ra.

Can - to al - la vi - ta al - la sua bel-lez - za.

LET ME FALL
from CIRQUE DU SOLEIL - QUIDAM

Words and Music by JIM CORCORAN
and BENOIT JUTRAS

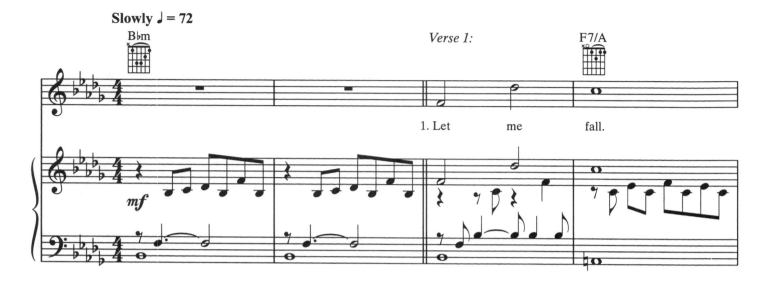

may not rise. I_____ will dance so

free - ly, hold - ing on__ to no one.

You_____ can hold me on - ly if you too will fall__ a-

way from all__ these use - less fears__ and shame.

VINCENT
(Starry, Starry Night)

Words and Music by
DON McLEAN

Moderate ballad ♩ = 92

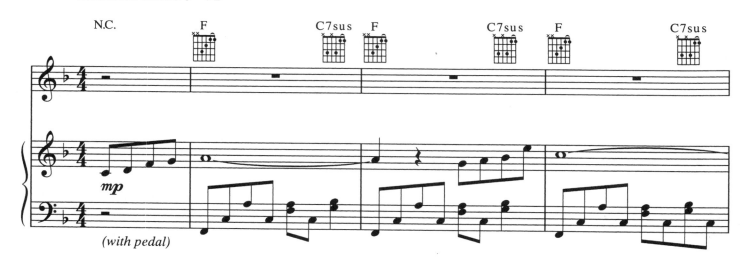

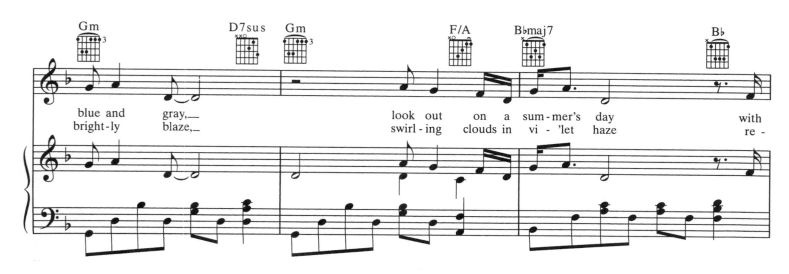

UN AMORE PER SEMPRE

Music by WALTER AFANASIEFF
Lyrics by MARCO MARINANGELI

HOME TO STAY

Words and Music by AMY FOSTER-SKYLARK
and JEREMY LUBBOCK

Slowly and gently, with expression (♩ = 60)

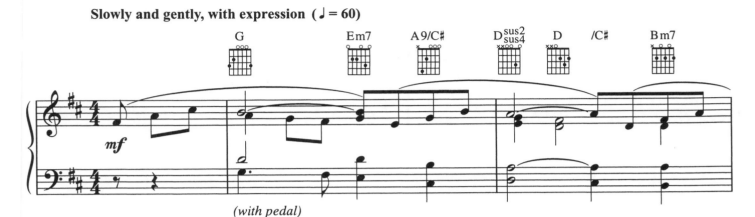

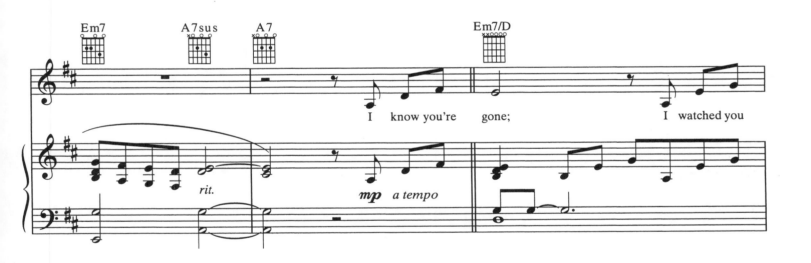

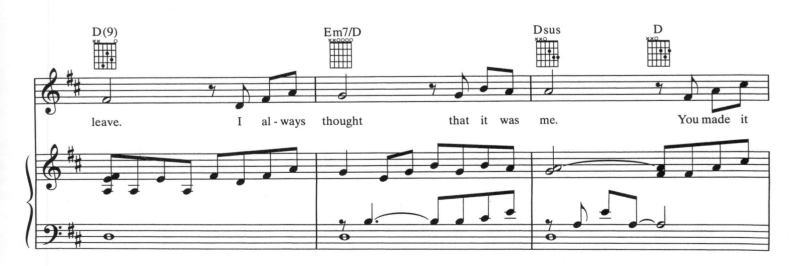

JESU, JOY OF MAN'S DESIRING

Arranged by DAVID FOSTER
and JEREMY LUBBOCK

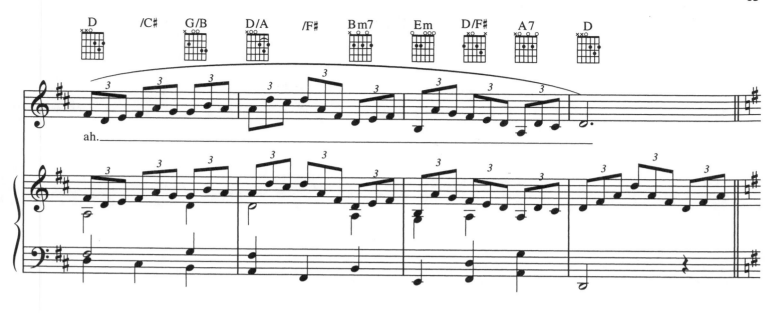

ah.

Male voice:

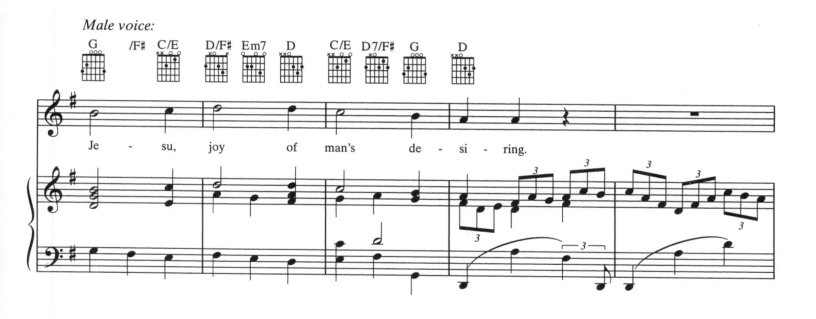

Je - su, joy of man's de - si - ring.

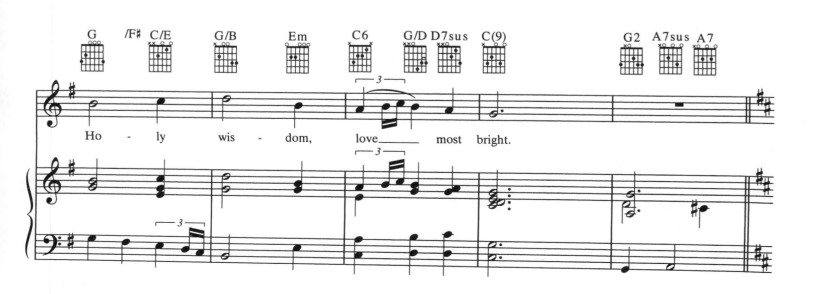

Ho - ly wis - dom, love_____ most bright.

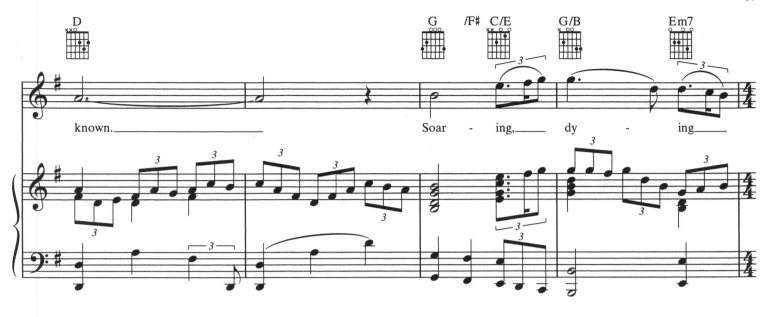

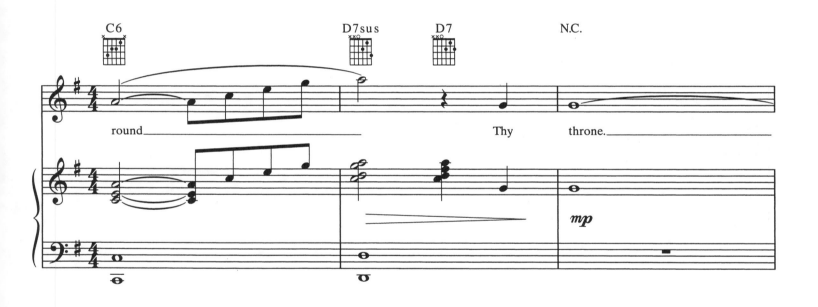

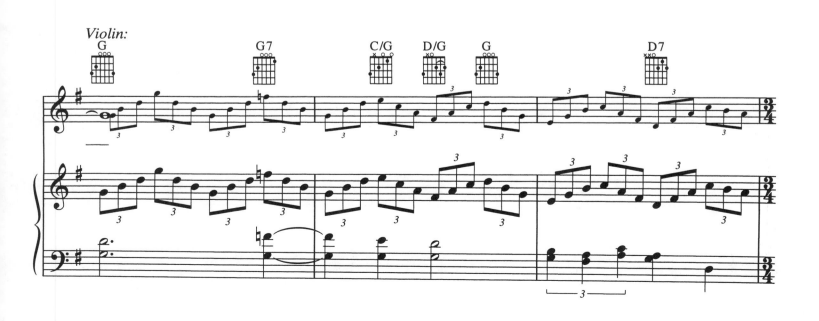

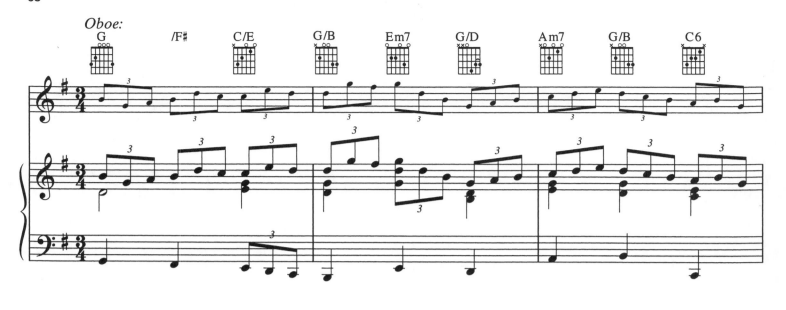

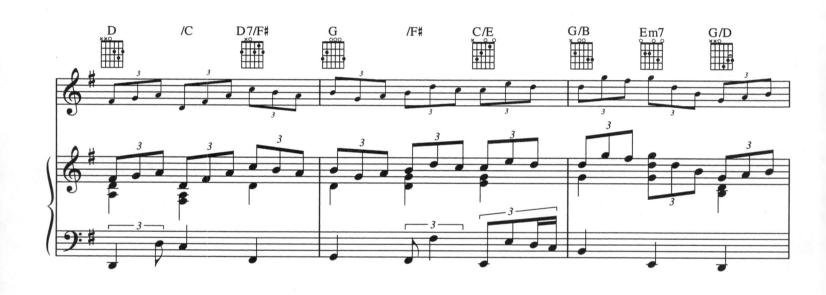

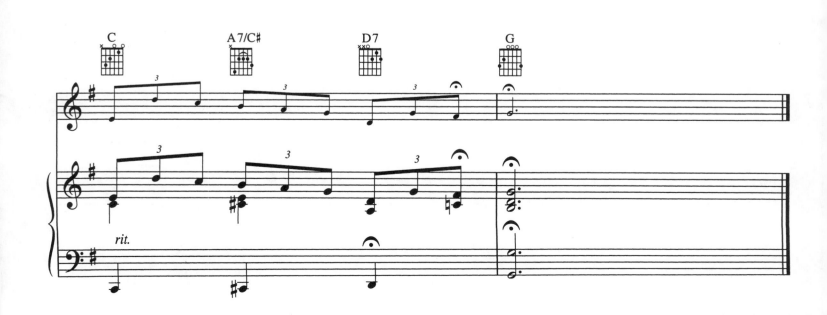

THE PRAYER

Words and Music by CAROLE BAYER SAGER
and DAVID FOSTER
Italian Lyrics by ALBERTO TESTA
and TONY RENIS

Slowly, with expression (♩ = 72)

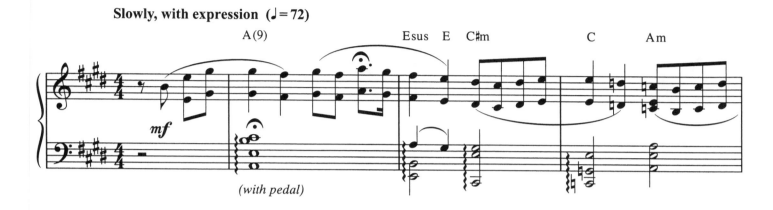

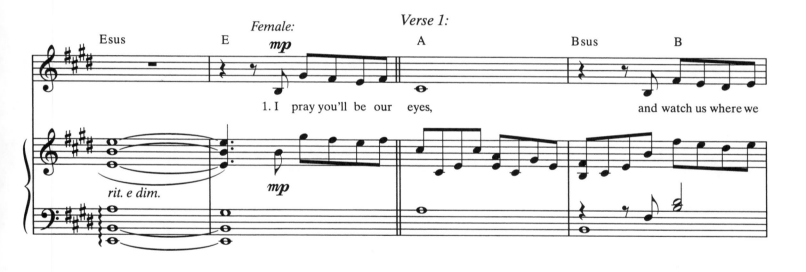

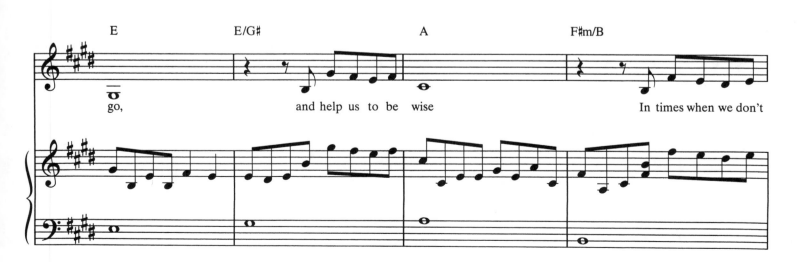

If there is one thing that is constant in this world, it is the Power of music. The songs in this book are very special to me as they have allowed me to share my inspirations, hopes, fears, sorrow and happiness with all of you. I can only wish that you enjoy them as much as I have.